ONE
Forever

ONE
Forever

*The transforming power of being **in Christ***

RORY SHINER

matthiasmedia
SYDNEY · YOUNGSTOWN

One Forever
Third edition
© Rory Shiner 2021

First edition 2012
Revised edition 2015

Matthias Media
(St Matthias Press Ltd ACN 067 558 365)
Email: info@matthiasmedia.com.au
Internet: www.matthiasmedia.com.au
Please visit our website for current postal and telephone contact information.

Matthias Media (USA)
Email: sales@matthiasmedia.com
Internet: www.matthiasmedia.com
Please visit our website for current postal and telephone contact information.

ISBN 978 1 925424 73 7

Cover design by Nicole Zhang.
Grid and series concept design by Annesa Fung.
Typesetting by Lankshear Design.

For Susan, of course.

CONTENTS

INTRODUCTION

The words we use to describe being a Christian are revealing.

I grew up in a Christian context where the dominant language was that of being *saved*. Others talk about making a *decision for Christ*. Sometimes the language is of *following* Christ. Most of us, somewhat prosaically, just speak of being *Christians* or *believers*.

In this book, I want to think about how the Bible, and especially the apostle Paul, describes being a Christian. Now, of course, all the descriptors above are true and biblical—we are *saved* by Christ (Eph 2:5), we *decide for* Christ (Col 2:6), we are called *Christians* (1 Pet 4:16), and we are *followers* of Jesus (1 Cor 11:1).

However, there is a phrase for our relationship with Christ that is everywhere in Paul's letters and almost nowhere in our churches. It is a phrase that towers over the rest in frequency, and it gives birth to some of the most vivid imagery of the New Testament. Yet we hardly ever use it.

Overwhelmingly, when the Bible wants to describe being a Christian, it says that we are *in Christ*.

The purpose of this book is to present the doctrine of being *in Christ* to people who, like me, are ordinary believers and who, also like me, have struggled to know what to do with this idea that theologians call 'union with Christ'.[1]

Why don't we talk like that?

Most of us (in my circles, at least) don't talk about being in Christ or united to Christ. Why is that?

Well, to be fair, it's just a hard idea to get your head around. I mean, what does it mean exactly to be *in* Christ, or for that matter, *in* anyone? If someone tells me I *follow* Christ, I get that. If someone says I am *under* Christ? Yep, I know what that means. *Saved by* Christ? Got it. *Inspired by?* Check. *Taught by?* Bingo. *In submission to?* I hear ya.

These are all concepts I understand and ideas for which I have ready analogies: Christ as a leader, a lord, a saviour, an inspiration, a teacher, a ruler. But to be *in Christ* almost seems to portray Christ as, well, a place, a sphere, a location—somewhere you can be. How does *that* work?

The concept of being 'in Christ' or 'united to Christ'

1   I want to thank Richard Chin and the Australian Fellowship of Evangelical Students for the invitation to first explore this topic in a series of talks at their National Training Event in Canberra in 2011.

was so new and so radical that Paul started inventing his own words to describe it. Before Paul, no-one had ever heard of being *co-crucified, co-buried, co-circumcised* or *co-raised* (Romans 6). Now in Christ, that is what has happened to all Christians.

The apostle John presents us with similar mind-bending ideas: that Christ is in the Father and we are in him and he is in us (John 14:20); and that in the incarnation, divinity and humanity—the creature and the Creator—should themselves become united in one person (John 1:14).

There may also be historical or temperamental reasons for not paying too much attention to the idea of being united to Christ. The very idea may strike many as too mystical, too subjective, too other-worldly. Or, tragically, it is just judged as too useless. If it's true that we are in Christ, what exactly are we supposed to do with that? What practical purpose does it serve?

In this book, I want us to follow some of the thinking of John, and especially Paul, regarding the believer's union with Christ. As we do so, we will discover that this doctrine—far from being impossible to grasp, subjective and impractical—is actually graspable, substantial, and, above all, deeply liveable.

Chapter 1

GLORY BE TO GOD FOR DAPPLED THINGS

Creation

Pied beauty
Glory be to God for dappled things—
    For skies of couple-colour as a brinded cow;
        For rose-moles all in stipple upon trout that swim;
Fresh-firecoal chestnut-falls; finches' wings;
    Landscape plotted and pieced—fold, fallow, and plough;
        And all trades, their gear and tackle and trim.
All things counter, original, spare, strange;
    Whatever is fickle, freckled (who knows how?)
            With swift, slow; sweet, sour; adazzle, dim;
He fathers-forth whose beauty is past change:
                    Praise him.

Gerard Manley Hopkins (1844-89)

Creation

Some filmmakers begin small and pan outward. The close-up of Bonasera's face as he makes his request in the dark, wood-panelled office of Vito Corleone is how Francis Ford Coppola chooses to begin his epic and sprawling tale of the rise and fall of the Corleone family in *The Godfather*.

Others choose to begin on a larger canvas before moving in toward their subject. Just think of the countless films about the lives of New Yorkers that begin with sweeping shots of the great city before focusing in on their subjects. Woody Allen's *Manhattan* comes to mind (or most Woody Allen films, for that matter).

The Bible is of the second type. It begins big: "In the beginning, God created the heavens and the earth" (Gen 1:1). And so I propose that before we narrow in on our topic of union with Christ, we start big—with the union of all things.

In the Genesis story, the six days of creation are not simply about God taking his time to do what is admittedly a big task—namely, creating the universe. Rather, they record a more intricate process of *creation*, *distinction* and *blessing*.

On the first day, God *creates* light. He then *distinguishes* light from darkness, then he *blesses* the distinction, calling it "good" (Gen 1:3-5). We see the same pattern with the sky and the sea (day two), and the sea and the land (day three): he *creates*, he *distinguishes*, and he *blesses* (Gen 1:6-13).

The places marked out in the first three days are the places God goes on to populate in the second three days. He fills the earth with animals, the seas with sea creatures, and the sky with birds (Gen 1:14-26).

Notice what's happened? The formless and empty world of Genesis 1:2—something that had unity of uniformity—becomes, under God's hand, a diverse unity. It is made good by each part being made different. Over the six days, it becomes a world where things aren't so much *like* each other as they are *for* each other. Like a wonderful machine, a complex ecosystem or a human body, the parts all fit each other.

This difference is the glory of creation. Fish are at their best when they are at their fishiest. Trees do their best work when they are most tree-like. All things glorify God by being most properly the things that they are: "It is no shame to a dog that it does not shine, or to a star that it does not bark".[2]

And the spaces God creates are the contexts for freedom. The sky is not the prison to which birds are banished, but the best place for their flourishing. An unhappy fish, making a sudden bid for freedom from the constrictions of the ocean and escaping to the land, will soon discover that the ocean was not its straitjacket, but its liberty.

2   NT Wright, *The Resurrection of the Son of God*, SPCK, London, 2004, p. 346.

Unity in diversity

At the apex of creation, on day six, God creates humanity: one entity in two forms as man and woman (Gen 1:27). Remember how God says, "Let *us* make man in our image" (Gen 1:26)? Who's the 'us' there? Is God talking to the angels? Is it a royal plural? Could be. But I don't think it's too much to see here a reference to what Christians call the Trinity: the unity and diversity of God himself—Father, Son and Spirit. The unity of humanity itself is, like creation, a unity in diversity. But maybe it is something that traces back to the very being of God himself, the one whose image they bear.

In Genesis 2, the wide-angle lens is replaced with a close-up. We are taken from the heavens into a garden, to the place where the man is to fulfil his role as God's image-bearer. The man is tasked with ruling over it in a way that brings it to its fullest expression.

In this context, God looks and makes an observation thousands have made since: when men are left alone to do a job, generally, it is "not good" (the last time I tried to change the tyre on our car being a case in point). The problem, at least in the first place, is not *loneliness*, but *aloneness*. It's not that he *feels* lonely, but that he *is* alone. And being alone—without diversity, without complement—is not a good way to bear God's image.

The problem is not sheer manpower. God is not worried about the heavy lifting that Adam will have to do. He does not just need another pair of hands or a 'second him', but someone other than him; someone who is like him, but distinct from him. Someone who, as we say in management speak, brings something else to the table.

And so God again embarks on a process of distinction. Having created Adam, he divides him. He takes the man and puts him into a deep sleep, and out of one of his ribs forms the woman. God the creator becomes God the surgeon, forming the woman out of the stuff of the man, who is now complete. And then God the surgeon finally becomes God the father of the bride. He takes the creature he has formed, the woman, and, like a proud father on the day of his daughter's wedding, presents her to the man (Gen 2:22).

In this scene, the first recorded words on human lips in the Bible are a love poem in praise of a woman:

> "This at last is bone of my bones
>> and flesh of my flesh;
> she shall be called Woman,
>> because she was taken out of Man." (Gen 2:23)

It is the poetry of recognition. He looks at her and says, "This one corresponds to me. She is one of my kind; bone of my bone and flesh of my flesh." But she is not just another version of him. They are not exactly the same as each other. They fit each other and complement each other.

And so in this moment, as Plato's Greek myth puts it, he finds his 'other half'. As Lana Del Ray says, he realizes that the world was meant for two. As Tom Cruise says to Renée Zellweger in *Jerry Maguire*, she completes him.

What's the point? In verse 24, the writer takes us aside and explains that this is the reason a man leaves his father and his mother and is united to his wife. That is, he leaves those who are *like* him—his family—to be united to one who is *unlike* him—a woman from a different family and different gender. Solidarity makes way for attraction, as attraction moves a man from those who are like him to the one to whom he is attracted by her difference. Why does this strange thing happen? As Genesis 2 explains, marriage is not just a union; it is a *re*union. It is not just a coming together, but also a coming *back* together of a unity (Adam) who became a diversity (Adam and Eve), and who enter now into a greater unity (one flesh).

Ephesians 5

Still feeling like we are a long way from our topic of union with Christ? We are closer than you might think. In the New Testament, in Ephesians 5, Paul says that Genesis 2 is ultimately about our union with Christ. The union of Adam and Eve is really a pointer to the union of Christ and his bride, the church: "This mystery is profound, and I am saying that it refers to Christ and the church" (Eph 5:32).

We have started at the beginning, not just because it is by all accounts a very good place to start, but because from here we can see that from its very opening words, the storyline of the Bible points to a goal of union with

Christ. And it points to a particular kind of union: not a unity of sameness, in which all things are conspiring and drawing together to become one thing, but a unity of complement, in which we and Christ (and ultimately all things, according to Ephesians 1:10) are being drawn together through the Messiah to a unity in diversity, a union in which each corresponds to the other. In our union with Christ by faith, we encounter (as Eve did in the garden, to take the bride's perspective) someone who is unlike us, but who, in being unlike us, corresponds to us in a way that someone who was exactly the same as us could never correspond. We discover that Christ is not us, nor is he a 'second us', but rather he is the completion of us. When we meet Christ by faith, it is not just a union. It is a reunion.

As the bride of Christ, he completes us and our reunion is a union.

Chapter 2

INTO THE FAR COUNTRY

Incarnation

...for us and for our salvation
he came down from heaven:
by the power of the Holy Spirit
he became incarnate from the Virgin Mary,
and was made man...

The Nicene Creed (381)

Have you ever noticed that our modern Christian holidays are celebrated almost in total inverse proportion to our theology? Christmas, the story of which takes up a total of two or three chapters of Matthew and Luke, is huge. Meanwhile Easter, the story of which is basically on every page of the New Testament, kind of stands as Christmas's poor cousin, with less food and no presents.

Emmanuel — God made flesh, united in likeness to us.

Why that is, and how we might change it, is a topic for another time. Most of this book is (I think rightly) concerned with the events we might file under 'Easter'—the death and resurrection of Jesus. But before we get there, we do need to think about the event we might file under 'Christmas'—not meaning, of course, presents and turkey, or even the details of Jesus' birth of which Luke and Matthew inform us. Rather, it is about the simple yet endlessly profound fact that in the birth of Jesus, God was made flesh. God was united to us.

According to the Bible, the Son of God took a journey into a far country.[3] The country was Creation, and he visited it not as a tourist on a temporary visa, but by becoming one of that country's citizens: "the Word became flesh and dwelt among us..." (John 1:14a).

What it means

When Christians say that "the Word became flesh", it is worth saying what we don't mean. We don't mean, for example, that God became a man instead of being God. We don't mean that God came disguised as a man but was not really a man. What is true for us—that we cease to be alive when we are dead, or cease to be in San Francisco when we are in Edinburgh—is not true of the Word. That is, in the incarnation, the Word was truly

3   I take this phrase from K Barth, *Church Dogmatics,* vol. 4, part 1, *The Doctrine of Reconciliation,* ed. GW Bromiley and TF Torrance, T&T Clark,, London, 2004, p. 157.

Fully God + fully man— real union

God and truly human *at the same time*. It was (and is) a real union.

Jesus was, in every conceivable sense, one of us. He ate and drank. He slept and talked. He had friendships and experienced grief and sorrow. He was, in short, like us in every respect (cf. Heb 2:17, 4:15), including temptation, and excluding only sin.

He truly came into the far country.

Why?

The Nicene Creed, from the year 381, says that it was "for us men and for our salvation" that he "became man". As the early Christians who eventually wrote the Nicene Creed worked out, the best way to think about the union of God and man is not at the level of metaphysics or abstract philosophy, but through the gospel. We begin to understand the incarnation when we understand that, in Jesus, God became man *for us*. From that vantage point, I think we can affirm at least three things.

1. Affirming our humanity...

First, by the Word becoming flesh, God reaffirms the purpose he gave humanity in the beginning.

As we saw in the previous chapter, humanity was commissioned by God to be his image-bearers to creation. Just as you can visit countries where a photograph of the ruling monarch adorns every public building, so too God's plan included an image of himself—us—within his creation. In making humanity, God wanted the creation to know the goodness of his rule by seeing the goodness of our rule.

Seen from this perspective, Christianity is surprisingly humanistic. It's not humanistic in the sense of humanity *instead of* God, of course. But it is humanistic in this sense: that God, the Creator of all things, became a human being. He "abhorred not the virgin's womb", says the Christmas carol. And he did not begrudgingly accept becoming a human being as a kind of necessary evil, the way we might accept becoming smelly when we decide to clean the contents of a spilt bin. On the contrary, as St Athanasius says, his presence in one human body brought dignity to every human.[4] The one whose image we bear came to bear our image. And in doing so, it is as if God said: "Plan A is for humanity to be my glory in the creation. There is no Plan B. Plan A was good."

Being human it not something to be ashamed of, but something to rejoice in. And God's purpose, as the incarnation makes clear, is not to abandon the project of being human, but to restore it to its full glory and goodness.

2. ...without flattering us

The union of God and man in the incarnation is affirming, but it is not flattering. His presence in flesh, his union with us, tells us that we are on the wrong track and we need redemption. It was not for us and for our

4   St Athanasius, *On the Incarnation*, trans. J Behr, SVS Press, New York, 2011, p. 50.

egos that God became one of us. It was "for us *and for our salvation*". And things only need saving when something has gone wrong—in our case, horribly wrong.

One of the problems early Christians struggled with is the fact that Jesus wasn't just a man in the abstract, but so very much a particular man. Almost to the point of embarrassment, he really was so very human. He had an ethnicity (Jewish), a hometown (Nazareth), and a gender (male). He was conceived out of wedlock. He was an undocumented asylum seeker in Egypt. He was tempted and tested. He was touched in a crowd and said, "Who touched my garments?" (Mark 5:30). He was deserted by his friends. He prayed, with tears, to his Father in heaven. He suffered, died and was buried.

If God really was going to become a man, would it honestly be *that* sort of man?

As the church grappled with this, they thought about big-picture issues like metaphysics, philosophy, ontology and epistemology. But they came back, again and again, to the raw content of the gospel. "Christ Jesus came into the world to save sinners…" (1 Tim 1:15). Jesus came "in the likeness of sinful flesh" (Rom 8:3) because *our* flesh was sinful. It is broken. Fallen. Rebellious. All the way down. The incarnation tells us that, too.

Why did God become man? St Gregory put it this way: "That which he did not assume he could not heal".[5]

5   St Gregory of Nazianzus, 'The first letter to Cledonius the Presbyter', trans. L Wickham, in *On God and Christ: The five theological orations and two letters to Cledonius*, SVS Press, New York, 2002, p. 158.

What he means is this: He, Jesus Christ, the Son of God, became all that we are, because *all that we are* needed saving. Our rebellion against God was no light thing: it was not something that affected just our minds, or just our hearts, or just our bodies. It affected everything.

And so in the incarnation, God doesn't enter into humanity like a nuclear scientist holds radioactive material: with a massive suit on, at a distance, for fear of contamination. Rather, he enters into all that we are and is united to all that we are, so that all that we are can be healed and redeemed.

3. Showing our future

The incarnation of the Son of God affirms that humanity is a good thing. But at the same time, it reminds us that our sinfulness goes all the way down. Finally, and gloriously, the incarnation shows us our future.

One of the poets of the Old Testament wrote a poem celebrating God's purpose for humanity. In the words of Psalm 8, he says:

> What is man that you are mindful of him,
>   and the son of man that you care for him?
> Yet you have made him a little lower than the heavenly
>   beings
>   and crowned him with glory and honour. (Ps 8:4-5)

In the New Testament, in the letter to the Hebrews, the writer picks up on this psalm and says, in effect, "I get it, but I don't see it! I get that that is our purpose, but I don't see us fulfilling that purpose." Speaking of humans, he says, "...we do not yet see everything in subjection to him" (Heb 2:8b). We don't see humanity as it ought to be...

> But we see him who for a little while was made lower
> than the angels, namely Jesus, crowned with glory
> and honour... (Heb 2:9)

In Jesus, we see the future of humanity. We see 'Humanity 2.0'. Humanity returned to and extended in its role as the glory of God and the image of God. And in the incarnation, we don't just see a blueprint, or an idea, or an aspiration. We see a person—a real human upon whom we can look and about whom we can say, "That's our future!"

The bedrock of this great mission of God—to send his Son into the far country for us and for our salvation—is the union of God and man. It is as God becomes flesh, as God makes his dwelling among us, that we are redeemed to be what we were meant to be.

And here's the strange and brilliant thing: this union will never end. The Son of God, who became flesh for us, remains and will always be, united to us. He is a man before God: the God-Man. He is the focal point and full realization of our destiny: to be united to our Creator.

in becoming flesh, God unites himself with all that we are, in order to redeem all that's gone wrong. He does it with us through Christ, rather than at arm's length.

Chapter 3

IN CHRIST YOU ARE A NEW CREATION

Salvation

> You are all one in Christ Jesus. (Gal 3:28b)

If in the incarnation the Son of God is united to us, then in salvation we are united to him. We are, to use Paul's favourite and often used phrase, "in him". But what exactly does that phrase mean?

Statement of fact

Strikingly, Paul is so at home with this "in Christ" phrase that he uses it reflexively, much as many of us might automatically tick the box for 'Christian' on a census form.

So, for example, in Romans 16:7, when Paul is listing people he wants to greet, he mentions Andronicus and Junia, his relatives, who were "in Christ before me". Or consider Ephesians 1, where Paul pours forth a torrent of blessings we have through the gospel. He tells us that we have every spiritual blessing (v. 3), that we have been chosen (v. 4), redeemed (v. 7) and given knowledge of the mystery of his will (v. 9), that we see God bringing all things together (v. 10), and that we have an inheritance (v. 11). Where do we have these things? Again and again, it is "in him". It is Paul's standard-issue way of saying 'Christian'.

Stuck to him

Elsewhere, the New Testament talks about the same idea, not by saying we are *in him*, but that we are sort of *stuck to him, united to him*. For example, Romans 6:6 says that we were *co-crucified* with Christ. Christ was glorified and we were glorified *with him* (Rom 8:17). We reign *with him* (2 Tim 2:12), we were made alive *with Christ* (Col 2:13) and we are hidden *with Christ* (Col 3:3).

The sacraments

Think for a moment about the Christian practices of baptism and the Lord's Supper. Have you ever noticed that both of them communicate some sort of union, some sort of participation? You don't just talk about the bread and the wine; you drink it—you take it into you.

And you don't just talk about baptism; you are immersed into the water—you go into it and rise from it. From the very first days of the faith, our symbols have not been symbols of mere assent, but symbols of participation, immersion and union.

Pictures of union

As well as phrases like "in Christ", the Bible uses vivid pictures of our union. Let's look at some examples:

- **The vine and the branches:** sometimes these are *agricultural images,* like in John's Gospel where Jesus says that he is the vine and we are the branches (John 15:5). It is a picture of organic connection with Jesus.
- **One flesh:** sometimes they are *sexual images*, like in Ephesians, where Paul says that we are, like a couple in marriage, made one flesh with Jesus. (Eph 5:32)
- **The body of Christ:** other times they are *biological images*, like in 1 Corinthians 12 where Paul says we are members of Christ's body.

All these images—the *in Christ* language, the *with Christ* language, the Christian practices of baptism and the Lord's Supper, the images of the vine, the marriage bed and the body—describe what theologians batch together under the label 'union with Christ.'

Being in Christ

If the plane arrived, I arrive :)

But again, what does it actually mean to be *in Christ*? Let me try an analogy. Imagine yourself at the airport, about to board a plane. The plane is on its way to, let's say, beautiful Perth. You're at the airport. There's you. There's the plane. It's going to Perth. And my question is: What relationship do you need to have with that plane?

Would it help, for example, to be *under* the plane? To submit yourself to the plane's eminent authority in the whole flying-to-Perth caper?

Would it help to be *inspired by* the plane? You go to the airport, you watch it take off, and you whisper to yourself, "One day, I could do that too..."?

What about *following* the plane? You know the plane is going to Perth, and so it stands to reason that if you take note of the direction it goes, and pursue it as fast as your little legs will carry you, you too will end up in Perth.

Of course, the key relationship you need with the plane is not to be under it, behind it or inspired by it. You need to be *in* it.

Why? Because by being in the plane, what happens to the plane will also happen to you.

The question "Did you get to Perth?" will be part of a larger question, "Did the plane get to Perth?" If the answer to the second question is yes, and if you were in the plane, then what happened to the plane will also have happened to you.

At its heart, the New Testament idea of being in Christ is something like that. What the New Testament is saying is that through faith in Jesus Christ, we become united to him. And we are in him, so that whatever is true of Jesus is also true of us.

Conversion

So how does all this work? Think of someone becoming a Christian. A person comes to church for a while. They listen to the teaching, they do a course explaining the gospel, or they read the Bible with a friend. In the fullness of time they are persuaded, and they become a Christian.

What just happened?

The apostle Paul puts that experience in these words: "If anyone is in Christ, he is a new creation" (2 Cor 5:17). Notice the language. Paul doesn't say, "If anyone is in Christ, they are *becoming* a new creation". He is not talking about a subjective experience, but an objective reality. That person is now in Christ, and as a consequence they are now a new creation. Christ is the firstfruits of the new creation (cf. 1 Cor 15:20, 23), and we share that new creation by being in him.

Saved from the judgement of God

God will judge the world for its rebellion and evil. Like a fire coming through a forest, God's judgement comes on sin and wickedness.

In the Australian bush, if a fire is heading your way, one survival technique is to actually start another fire.

safe from fire

BURNED

It seems totally counter-intuitive—fire is the problem, so why start another one? Well, the logic is simple: if you burn out a patch of forest, then, when the bushfire comes, it cannot burn what has already been burned. By being in an already-burned patch of forest, the coming fire will not harm you.

Christ's death is like that with the coming judgement of God. Psalm 2 says of the Messiah, "Blessed are all who take refuge in him" (Ps 2:12b). In his death on the cross, Christ becomes the place of refuge, the place in the world where the full wrath of God has already been spent. Therefore, to stand in Christ is to stand in a place where the wrath of God will never be felt, because it has already been there.

The Belfast child

Before we are *in Christ*, we are, in the Bible's language, *in Adam* (Romans 5, 1 Corinthians 15). It's an odd, but not impossible, way to think of things.

I was born and have lived most of my life in Western Australia. And Western Australia is very hot. And I live there even though I suffer from a skin condition caused by a mutated gene called SLC-24-A5. It is a genetic deformity that makes my skin lose its pigmentation and become a kind of pasty pink colour. The condition (often coupled with an inability to dance) is commonly known as 'being white'. You may know other people with the same problem.

So the question is: How did such a person, so eminently unsuited to living in such a sunny place as Perth, end up there?

The reason (at least in part) is that my ancestors come from a place where the condition wasn't such a liability—namely, Northern Ireland. Many years ago, my grandfather (then a boy) boarded a boat from Belfast to Fremantle. He set up home in a Subiaco townhouse, west of Perth city. Eventually he met a lady called Lorna Brown (a fellow sufferer of the SLC-24-A5 mutation, as it happens), and they had four children including Alison, my mother.

Why am I in Western Australia? Well, to use the biblical language, I am in Western Australia because I was *in my grandfather*. In a sense, I was in Belfast. I was on that boat. I was in that townhouse. And it is because I was in him that my otherwise inexplicable circumstances (a pasty white boy living in a sun-drenched city) make sense. It's the clue that unlocks who I am and why things are as they are.

And that is what our relationship with Adam is like. At one level, I wasn't there in the garden of Eden. I didn't listen to the snake. I didn't initiate the rebellion. But in another sense I *was* there—because I was *in him*.

Just as my physical circumstances are incomprehensible apart from reference to my grandfather, so too my spiritual circumstances are incomprehensible apart from reference to my being in my great, great grandfather: Adam.

"Man", as Jean Paul Sartre said, "is a being to whom

something happened".[6] According to the Bible, what happened is that our father rebelled against God. As Romans 5 points out, the achievement of Adam was enormous in its scope. My grandfather's decision to get on a boat has affected about 50 or so direct descendants; Adam's decision to eat the fruit has affected about 7 billion people alive today. It has had impressive reach.

The gospel declares Jesus to be the last Adam (1 Cor 15:45). And the Bible promises that to be in Christ is to be implicated in something much vaster and grander and better than what happened to us by being in the first Adam. In short, being in Adam gave us death; but being in Christ gives us life: "As in Adam all die, so also in Christ shall all be made alive" (1 Cor 15:22).

Adam's achievement was, in a sense, an accident; Christ's achievement is deliberate. Adam grasped at life, and gave us all death; Christ did not grasp at life, but became obedient to death (cf. Phil 2:8) and gave us all life. Adam acted in disobedience; Christ acted in complete, perfect obedience. If Adam could achieve something so huge by doing something so incredibly dumb, how much more can Christ achieve something even bigger by doing something so incredibly good (cf. Rom 5:15-19)?

We are a new creation in the sense that we are in Christ, and Christ is the site of God's new creation. Indeed, Paul says that the rest of creation is waiting in longing for our liberation from our bondage to decay

6   Quoted in H Blocher, *Original Sin: Illuminating the Riddle,* Apollos, Leicester, 1997, p. 102.

(Rom 8:21). It is as if every time someone responds to the gospel, the rest of creation—every flower and drop of water and bunny rabbit and mountain range—gasps in anticipation, saying: "One more! One more! Praise God, our freedom is drawing closer!"

When someone does that simple act of putting their faith in Christ, the whole cosmos moves with them.

St Augustine

When Augustine, the great early church father, was converted, he had been living a wild life. He was involved in a cult. He was a promiscuous, unfaithful womanizer, given to drunkenness and debauchery. After a long struggle with God, he was eventually converted when he found a Bible open at Romans 13, where he read these words: "Let us walk properly as in the daytime, not in orgies and drunkenness, not in sexual immorality and sensuality, not in quarrelling and jealousy. But put on the Lord Jesus Christ..." (vv. 13-14).

When I first heard that story, I thought, "What a strange part of Romans to turn to!" I mean, of all the parts of Romans you could be in—Romans 3, Romans 4, Romans 5, Romans 6, Romans 8—why end up in Romans 13?

But the more I've thought about it, the more I think it's a brilliant verse. What is it to be a Christian? It is to *put on* the Lord Jesus Christ. It is to believe *into* him. It is to clothe yourself with him. To be a Christian is to be *in Christ*.

Back to the airport

Come back with me to the airport. Imagine now that there is not one person heading to Perth, but two.

The first is a businesswoman who flies from Melbourne to Perth every month for board meetings with her oil and gas company. She gets to the airport with 20 minutes to spare and goes straight through to the lounge to re-caffeinate and grab a copy of the *Financial Review* before boarding. When boarded, she barely lifts her eyes from the paper as the hostess tells the passengers what to do in the case of a non-traditional landing. She could probably recite the thing by heart anyway.

The second is an old man who is getting into a plane for the first time in his life, his family having pooled their resources together to fulfil his lifelong dream of seeing the sun set over the Indian Ocean. He's at the airport two hours early. He studies the plane from the viewing deck, marvelling at the thought that this massive machine—made of iron!—could ever take to the skies. When boarded, he not only listens to the safety instructions but also takes notes, which he will review at regular intervals during the flight. As the plane takes off, his palms become clammy and his heart doubles its activity, preparing his nervous body for a fight or (quite literally) flight response. Throughout the whole trip, he is full of wonder and fear, and at several points presses the buzzer to ask the hostess: "Are you *sure* everything is going to be okay?"

Two important questions:

- First: who has more faith? Answer: The woman. She is a model of total trust in the plane and its pilots. The old man, on the other hand, is full of doubt.
- But second: Who makes it to Perth? Answer: Both of them! Why? Because the strong faith of the woman or doubting faith of the man has very little to do with it. It has everything to do with the plane. At this point, the question is not, "Who believes more?" but "Where are you?" If you are in the plane, then the amount of faith you have in the plane has nothing to do with whether or not you make it to Perth.

Being in Christ is a very similar reality. The heart of the matter is not how much faith you have, but where your faith is.

Now of course, there may be such a person who looks at the plane, gets back in the taxi and heads home. Like the old man, this one also has their doubts. But in the case of the old man, he has the faith that matters: he has faith enough to get into the plane, and consequently he makes it to Perth.

One of the many wonderful things being in Christ does is give us a knowledge of salvation that takes our eyes off ourselves and puts them on him. When we understand that the foundation of our salvation is to be found in him, then we know that it is not faith in the abstract, or the amount of faith, that will save us, but it is the one in whom we have our faith. We are saved *in him*.

If in incarnation, God is united to us then in salvat[n], we are united to him. p29

You are all one in Christ Jesus (Gal 3: 28)

in Christ = Christian, Rom 16:7
glorified with him
reign with him
alive with Christ
hidden in Christ
Drink communion (in) & (immersed) in baptism
One flesh - Eph 5
Body of Christ - 1 Cor 13
Vine & branches - J 15

The Plane
- if plane going to Perth & you're in it, you'll arrive
- admiring, being under its power or following aren't enough, you need to be in it.
- whether you're full of faith or doubting, if you're in the plane & in Christ, you'll arrive.
- as those in Christ, we are saved from the wrath of God. as its already been there. its like standing in a burned out patch to escape a forest fire.
- Being in Adam & in Christ explain our spiritual circumstances

Chapter 4

BEFORE THE THRONE OF GOD ABOVE

Justification

Before the throne of God above,
I have strong, a perfect plea...

Charitie L Bancroft (1863)

Suspicious minds

We moderns are a rather suspicious lot. We are trained from childhood to be suspicious of everything, to trust no-one. Some of the great thinkers of the modern age—Marx, Freud and Einstein—are even called the masters of suspicion. Einstein taught us that the world is not as it looks, Freud that our desires are not as innocent as we suppose, and Marx that society is arranged for exploitation.

We are taught to read suspiciously. We learn at high school to be aware of Thomas Hardy conforming us to patriarchal narratives, that Shakespeare is conditioning our response to The Other, and that Christopher Robin is alienating Winnie and Tigger from the means of production.

And, ever since the snake made his suspicious suggestion back in the garden—"Did God *actually* say..." —we have been suspicious of God. Is God really good? Is God really for us?

How does being in Christ help to deal with our suspicious minds?

Union with Christ and justification

Union with Christ is not just one of the things we get, along with adoption, forgiveness and hope. Union with Christ is also the means by which we get the whole package. All the blessings of Christ are ours because we are in Christ. Understanding things in this way makes a material difference to many things, not least our understanding of justification. In particular, as we will see, it addresses our suspicions and grants us assurance.

Justification

What is justification? Justice[7] is a characteristic of God himself. To say that God is just draws attention to God as our judge; it is to say that his judgements are perfect. God will find in favour of the innocent and condemn the guilty. He is a righteous judge (Gen 18:25). The state of justification, then, is to be declared right. It is to be found innocent—not guilty—before the righteous court of God (Rom 5:1).

Justification is never less than that, but it is more than that. For the Bible promises that God will bring justice to the whole creation (Eph 1:10). At the moment, the world is like a computer or phone app that is out of sync with its internet-based 'cloud'. But in the Lord's Prayer, when we pray "your will be done, on earth as it is in heaven" (Matt 6:10), we are praying that heaven and earth will one day be synced again. That is justice.

The doctrine of justification makes a claim that is, on the surface, confusing: namely, that God is both just (he always makes the right call) and he justifies (declares to be not guilty) those who have faith in Christ Jesus (Rom 3:26). Given our sinfulness and God's righteousness, it would seem impossible for God to be able to do both. To be just would seem to require condemnation of the guilty sinner (cf. Exod 23:7), and to declare the guilty innocent would seem to undermine the claim that his

---

7   Or righteousness—they are both the same word in the Greek in which the New Testament was written.

Only because we're in Christ, can we be justified + God be just.

judgements are just. However, in the cross of Christ, God has opened up a way to be the first and do the second—a way, that is, of being both just and the one who justifies those who have faith in Christ Jesus (Rom 3:26). He declares us justified *through Christ*, by setting forth his Son as a sacrifice of atonement. In the death of Jesus sin is rightly condemned, but the sinner is justified and the character of God is shown to be perfectly just.

Justification and union

I have only briefly summarized the doctrine of justification, because my concern is to explore the doctrine in relation to union with Christ. Of that connection, John Calvin says this:

> As long as Christ remains outside of us, and we are separated from him, all that he has suffered and done for the salvation of the human race remains useless and of no value to us.[8]

Justification is objective. Justification is something that happens *for* us rather than *to* us. My justification was achieved not in my heart, but on a cross outside Jerusalem.

But Calvin pushes further. He says, in effect, here is Christ: his life of obedience to the Father, his death

8   J Calvin, *The Institutes of the Christian Religion*, vol. 1, book 3, trans. FL Battles, Westminster Press, Philadelphia, 1960, p. 537.

for sins, his vindication in his resurrection and his ascension to the right hand of the Father. And here are we: early 21st-century human rebels against God. Of what use is Christ's work of justification to us? Answer: none. It is of no value to us, *so long as Christ remains outside of us.*

In other words, Calvin is saying that there is no justification apart from union with Christ.

In 2 Corinthians 5:21, Paul says, "For our sake [God] made him to be sin who knew no sin, so that in him we might become the righteousness of God". Notice the language. Christ is made sin for us. And we *become* the righteousness of God. How does that happen? Here comes that now-familiar phrase: it happens *in him.*

Or consider Philippians 3:8-9. Having just talked about his brilliant spiritual CV, Paul says of his achievements:

> For his sake I have suffered the loss of all things and count them as rubbish, in order that I may gain Christ and be found *in him,* not having a righteousness of my own that comes from the law, but that which comes through faith in Christ, the righteousness from God that depends on faith.

Remember that plane to Perth? Sometimes justification is wrongly spoken of as if some frequent flyer points have been mysteriously credited to your account, giving the *appearance* that you made it to Perth, though in reality you remain in Melbourne. It is what people call a 'legal fiction'. But biblically, justification is not a legal fiction. Just as the passengers on that plane really do get to Perth, those who have faith in Christ really are justified before the Father, because they are (you guessed it) *in him*.

Justification, union and the suspicious mind

Justification is one of the great joy factories of the Christian life. When there is no joy (cf. Gal 4:15), it is often a telltale sign that we have lost our grasp on this doctrine. The suspicion that characterized our relationship with God before we knew him in Christ starts to creep back in and take over.

Paul, with the suspicious mind firmly in his sights, addresses our fears in Romans 8.

In verse 31 he begins: "What then shall we say to these things?" Paul is thinking back over what he has said in Romans 8 so far. There is now no condemnation for those who are *in Christ Jesus* (v. 1). We have received the Spirit, who testifies to our spirit that we are the children of God (v. 15). Our present suffering is not worth comparing to the glory that will be revealed to us (v. 18). All things work together for the good of those who love God and are called according to his purpose (v. 28). Those God foreknew he also predestined to be conformed to the image of his son (v. 29). And those that God predestined he also called, and those he called he also justified, and those he justified he also glorified (v. 30).

Paul gathers all those truths together and he says, "What then shall we say to these things?" And he responds with a series of questions and answers.

Question 1: "If God is for us, who can be against us?" (v. 31)

Notice the premise: God is for us.

It's amazing what you can cope with when you know someone is for you. I can think of situations in my own life where the difference between coping and going under was knowing that someone, sometimes even just one person, was on my side.

Paul says that in Christ, the God of the universe is *for* us. God is on our side. And so he asks the question: "If God is for us, who can be against us?"

Of course, all sorts of people *can* be against you. But what he's asking is this: if God is for you, whose 'against you' actually counts? Your boss's? Your family's? Your government's? Your own? Whose 'against you' is more powerful than God's 'for you'? The answer, of course, is "No-one's". Not your boss's, not your family's, not Satan's, not even your own. Nothing and no-one can undo God's decision to be for you.

Question 2: "He who did not spare his own Son but gave him up for us all, how will he not also with him graciously give us all things?" (v. 32)

Again, notice the premise: God did not spare his own Son. For your sake and for mine, God willingly gave that which was most precious to him. Do you think it's now possible that he would ultimately withhold good things from you? He was willing to give over his own beloved Son. Is it really likely that in any other area of life his plan is to be stingy and withholding? Really?

Question 3: "Who will bring any charge against God's elect?" (v. 33)

Like a prize-fighter in a boxing ring, Paul stands up and says: "Here is the one God has justified. Do we have any challengers? Is anyone willing to bring a charge against those God has chosen?" And the would-be challengers fall silent. No charges can be brought.

Question 4: "It is God who justifies. Who is to condemn?" (vv. 33-34)

In the face of God's "Yes", would anyone like to try a "No"? As JI Packer once put it, God justified us with his eyes open.[9] He knew the worst about us, but even so, in Christ he did not condemn us but justified us.

And if that is the case, then it follows that no-one—not your enemies, not Satan, not even yourself—can produce charges that will persuade him to reverse his decision. As if God is suddenly going to go, "Oh my goodness, I had no idea they were like *that*!"

Paul can only entertain one possible person who could bring a charge against you: Jesus Christ. He alone in the universe might be able to seek a review of the court's findings. But what is Christ doing? Having died for us, he is now at the right hand of the Father *interceding for us.*

9   JI Packer, *Knowing God,* Hodder and Stoughton, London, 1973, p. 301.

We are in Christ & inseparable

Question 5: "Who shall separate us from the love of Christ?" (v. 35)

Paul's answer, once again, is "No-one". No-one and nothing comes close to being able to do that.

Now, Paul could have just left it at that. But he knows how suspicious minds work. He knows that our minds go to the loophole, the exception, the 'out' clause. And so he spells it out for us, step by step.

Could famine or nakedness or sword separate us? No.

Could life or death separate us? No.

What about angels and demons? Could they separate us from the love of God? No.

The present? No.

The future? No.

And just in case our minds think of something that Paul hasn't included, some little escape clause, some tiny wedge that he has sneakily left off by which you could be separated from the love of God, Paul finishes his catalogue by saying, "nor anything else in all creation, will be able to separate us from the love of God in Christ Jesus our Lord" (v. 39).

Do this with me for a moment. In your imagination, picture *everything*. Everything in the whole universe. I'll just give you a minute to make sure you get everything in there. Every demon, every angel. Every decision, every star, every circumstance. Every dress, every buffet. Every emotion, every success, every failure. Every ant and flower and spider and stone fruit. Every planet and solar system and black hole. Don't miss anything out. Your ex-girlfriend. Your fourth grade teacher. Mental illness. Failing an exam. Car crashes. Marriage problems.

Got everything? Good.

Paul is saying that *nothing* you just thought of could, will ever, can ever separate you from the love of God, which is where? *In Christ Jesus our Lord.*

Conclusion

In his now-famous speech of 2005 to a group of university students in the United States, the author David Foster Wallace—not, as far as I know, a Christian—said this:

> Anything else you worship will eat you alive. If you worship money and things—if they are where you tap real meaning in life—then you will never have enough... Worship your own body and beauty and sexual allure and you will always feel ugly, and when time and age start showing, you will die a million deaths before they finally plant you.[10]

Wallace was not speaking as a Christian, but he speaks a deeply biblical truth. Whenever we look for justification, significance and security in things other than in Christ, those things will eat us up.

But in Christ, in union with him, we find that place in the universe where we are justified before the Father—that place where we can never, ever be separated from the love of God. That's a good place to be.

10 DF Wallace, 'This is Water', *The Guardian*, 20 September 2008.

Chapter 5

IN WHICH WE FACE SOME PLAYGROUND BULLIES

Union and sin

Holiness

Union with Christ is a great doctrine of assurance and hope and peace. But, you may well ask, is it of any help on, say, a Tuesday afternoon when you're out there battling the challenges of life? Maybe you're grappling with bitterness or anger. Maybe you're addicted to porn, and that overshadows everything else in your Christian life. Maybe you just can't prise yourself from that obsession to have what the other guy has. What, if anything, does union with Christ have to say about *that*?

Does it help us with the vast dangers that lie in wait—the dangers of sin and temptation?

As it happens, far from being out of its depth in these areas, the doctrine of union with Christ is precisely the doctrine Paul calls on when it comes to actually living the Christian life, overcoming sin and growing in holiness. It is as if the doctrine of union with Christ sees those things and yells to us, "Kick it to me! Kick it to me! That's what I do!"

Union with Christ is our defence against the playground bullies of sin and temptation.

You can see the logic of union with Christ and holiness worked out all over the New Testament, but nowhere more clearly than in Romans 6.

By the time we get to Romans 6, we are pretty sure what *won't* help in the battle with sin. We can't do it, and the law can't do it. It is grace, not the law, that overcomes our guilt before God. Indeed, in a strange way, grace grows where sin grows (5:20).

This leads to the obvious question: "Are we to continue in sin that grace may abound?" (Rom 6:1) Or in verse 15: "Are we to sin because we are not under law but under grace?"

For Paul, sin is a power; it *reigns*. And grace is a power; it also *reigns*. But who wins? Is grace kind of like a relief teacher on muck-up day? She says to the class, "*Please* don't do that", but we all know she doesn't have any real clout. Is that grace—something that 'reigns' in the sense that a relief teacher 'reigns' over a bunch of school-leavers who can smell freedom?

We died

Paul's answer to the potential clash of these two powers, sin and grace, is simple: we died. "How can we who died to sin still live in it?" (Rom 6:2). When did we die? "Do you not know that all of us who have been baptized *into Christ Jesus* were baptized into his death?" (v. 3).

What comes to mind for you when you think of baptism? Depending on your denominational background, you might associate baptism with babies and flowers, kids in white dresses and family reunions. Or baptism for you might conjure up visions of friends and family gathered at a beach or a swimming pool to witness the occasion. Either way, baptisms are typically (and rightly) happy occasions.

But notice what Paul does with baptism here. Your baptism was your funeral. Now, unless something goes horribly wrong, you should survive your baptism and make it to the supper afterwards. But the point of the baptism imagery is that in it we participate in the death of Jesus. We die because we died *with him*: "All of us who have been baptized into Christ Jesus were baptized into his death" (v. 3).

Just as to go under the water is to symbolically die with Christ, to come out of the water is to be raised with Christ. "We were buried therefore with him by baptism into death"—why?—"in order that, just as Christ was raised from the dead by the glory of the Father, we too might walk in newness of life" (v. 4).

One of the crucial truths that union with Christ

captures is that *all* of me is connected to *all* of Christ.

If we only think of ourselves as following Christ, or trusting Christ, or knowing Christ, or being near Christ, then we don't capture what union captures: that all we are is connected to all Christ is and all he has done. "Our old self was crucified with him in order that the body of sin might be brought to nothing" (v. 6).

By being in Christ, our old selves were *crucified* with Christ. Sometimes we think that our old self, our flesh, received a kind of non-fatal beating. At best it sustained some serious injury, and at worst it got away with a Monty Python-esque round with some fluffy pillows.

But the truth is that by union with Christ, our old self —the self that stood under the just judgement of God— was *crucified* with Christ. That self is simply no longer in play. It died with Christ. *We* died with Christ.

In verse 7, Paul puts this in the language of freedom from slavery. If sin is a master, then it is by participation in the death of Christ Jesus that we are released from the slave master of sin, "for one who has died has been set free from sin".

For those not acquainted with John Owen, he is a rather intimidating figure. For starters, he was a Puritan —and when you hear the word 'puritan', you don't immediately think, "Man, those guys lived for pleasure!" Aren't they the ones who, like the White Witch of Narnia, tried to get rid of Christmas?

John Owen wrote books with catchy titles like, *The Death of Death in the Death of Christ: A treatise in which the whole controversy about universal redemp-*

tion is fully discussed. And that's not even the subtitle. And with his other book titles like *The Mortification of Sin*, it all sounds a bit… well, severe.

But listen to John Owen's words on overcoming sin. What do you think this seemingly hard-nosed Puritan is going to say about the hindrances to our holiness?

> When men can live and plod on in their profession, and not be able to say when they had any living sense of the love of God or of the privileges which we have in the blood of Christ, I know not what they can have to keep them from falling into snares.[11]

Notice what he says? Without knowing the love of God, without knowing the privileges we have *in Christ*, we cannot be kept from falling into the snares of temptation. As someone else has put it: "Our greatest hindrance in the Christian life is not our lack of effort, but our lack of acquaintedness with our privileges".[12]

Guilt, you see, is a good alarm system. It does a wonderful job of alerting us to what's wrong. But while it may be a good alarm system, it's a lousy agent for change. The problem is that many of us think that because guilt alerted us to the problem, it will also help to get us out of

11   J Owen, *The Works of John Owen,* vol. 6, ed. WH Goold, Banner of Truth, London, 1966, p. 134.
12   I Hamilton, 'The Cross of Christ', transcription of a lecture given at a public meeting of the Inverness branch of the Scottish Reformation Society, Inverness, 14 November 2005 (accessed 3 December 2012): http://www.reformation-scotland.org.uk/articles/cross-of-christ.php

the problem. But it can't. So what is the solution? Only a greater acquaintance with the privileges of Christ can free us from the snares of sin.

So the proper approach to overcoming sin is not to ratchet up the guilt, but to claim our identity as those united to Christ. Look how Paul expresses it in Romans 6: "So you also must consider yourselves dead to sin and alive to God in Christ Jesus" (v. 11).

Paul says: In Christ, you are dead to sin; you are free from sin. Therefore, live it out. Be who you are!

Freedom from slavery

The great Welsh preacher, Martyn Lloyd-Jones, explains it with this illustration. On 18 December 1865, Abraham Lincoln's Secretary of State William Seward declared an end to the institution of slavery in the United States of America. There, at that moment, legally and in reality, slavery in America was over.

But facts and feelings don't always coincide.

Imagine you were raised in slavery. You had only ever known life as a slave. Then suddenly, on December 18, it's over. You are not a slave any more—you're free. But the next day, as you are walking down the street some-where in Alabama, you hear the voice of your old master call out, "Boy! Come here."

Suddenly, years of the experience of slavery come flooding into your mind. Do you feel like his slave again? Yes! But does that feeling make you his slave? No!

That is just like what union with Christ does to us and sin. In the gospel, our freedom is declared. It is a reality. It has happened. And as those who are in Christ, our battle begins in the mind: we consider ourselves, *reckon* ourselves, dead to sin, because that is the reality of what we are in Christ. Like Bilbo about to meet Smaug in the cave, the real battle begins in the mind, at that point where we reckon ourselves dead to sin.

And so, just as the former slave has to consciously think, "That man no longer owns me", so too, when we hear temptation's voice, we are to think, "No, sin no longer owns me".

In 1 Corinthians 6, Paul addresses members of the church in Corinth who are visiting prostitutes. What does he say to them to bring about their repentance?

> Do you not know that your bodies are members of Christ? Shall I then take the members of Christ and make them members of a prostitute? Never! Or do you not know that he who is joined to a prostitute becomes one body with her? (1 Cor 6:15-16)

Union with Christ, far from being something that a few select Christians can conjure up in their best moments, is actually something so real and so true that it's a reality you can't get rid of, even when you are united to a prostitute. To be united to a prostitute is to deny what is actually the case—that we *are* united to Christ.

Appeal to sinners as those united to Christ, and dead to sin. Baptised, we died with him & sin is no longer our master.

Christians aren't just forgiven

You've probably seen the popular bumper sticker that reads, "Christians aren't perfect, just forgiven". As a statement, it gets two things right and one thing horribly wrong.

It says Christians aren't perfect, which is demonstrably true. It says Christians are forgiven, which is also true. But it has that terrible little word 'just'. That's not true. It's not true that Christians are *just* forgiven Christians are forgiven, *and they are united to Christ*. They are indwelt by the Spirit of God, and they are empowered by God to live a new life. To fail to understand that reality is to leave ourselves open to a wildly inadequate approach to sin in our lives.

Holiness revisited

The truth is that, even for Christians, the presence of sin remains. Be under no illusions here: sin will remain in Christians until the new creation. However, while sin may remain, we must not let sin reign: "Let not sin therefore reign in your mortal body" (Rom 6:12). Sin's evil desires will still make their claims on us, but they must not be allowed to take charge.

Consider this in an actual encounter with the playground bullies of sin and temptation. Think about that moment when you receive a juicy bit of gossip, and everything in your body is telling you: "I have to pass this on".

Or consider the money that you have prayerfully put

aside for East Africa, but before it is sent you get an offer for a phone upgrade, which happens to cost about the same as the amount you have put aside.

Or the moment late at night when the Facebook newsfeed starts to dry up, and you could go to bed or go in search of porn.

It seems to me that in those moments, and a thousand others like them, it makes all the difference in the world whether you think you're *just* forgiven. In fact, you are to consider yourself "dead to sin but alive to God in Christ Jesus".

Apart from union with Christ, sin comes barking its orders. It says to you: "You know you're greedy, you know you're impure, you *are* a gossip—that's how you roll". But faith in Christ and union with him has changed not just your status but also your identity. If by faith in Christ you have actually died to sin with Christ, if your old self has actually been done away with, if you are actually risen with Christ to new life and new power, then you can say to that sin, to that temptation: "No! That's not who I am. To do what you are suggesting would be a contradiction of what God has made me in Christ."

Chapter 6

UNITED TO THE BODY OF CHRIST

Church

Anyone who is to find Christ must first find the church.
How could anyone know where Christ is and what faith
is in him unless he knew where his believers are?

Martin Luther

According to the Australian Bureau of Statistics, 61%
of Australians identify as Christian.[13] A Neilsen Poll
of 2009 found that a pretty neat 50% claimed to be
specifically Christian in what they believe—that Jesus

---

13   Australian Bureau of Statistics (ABS), 'Cultural diversity in Australia'
in *Reflecting a Nation: Stories from the 2011 Census, 2012-2013,* ABS
cat. no. 2071.0, ABS, Belconnen, 2012 (accessed 28 November 2012):
abs.gov.au/ausstats/abs@.nsf/Lookup/2071.0main+features902012-2013

was actually the Son of God, and so on.[14] An older poll from the late 1990s found that 43% of Australians believe that Jesus rose from the dead.[15]

That's strange, because Australia doesn't feel like a country that has been saturated with the joy-giving, life-changing, loneliness-quashing, hope-filling, creation-affirming message of Christ died and risen again.

There is much one could say and speculate about with those sorts of statistics. But whatever else they might mean, one thing they do tell us is that people don't go to church even when they believe (or claim to believe) what the churches teach. In 2003, only 19% of Australians went to church with any frequency at all.[16]

Journalist David Marr, who has no bias toward Christians, says that Australians are a very religious people who overwhelmingly believe in God, who fairly solidly believe in the Christian God, but who do not believe in church.[17]

So, here's my question: If all those people really were

14   D Marr, 'Our faith today', *The Sydney Morning Herald,* 19 December 2009.

15   National Christian Life Survey Research (NCLS Research), *Attender Beliefs and Practices,* NCLS Research, Strathfield, 2009 (accessed 28 November 2012): ncls.org.au/default.aspx?sitemapid=31

16   NCLS Research, *Who Goes to Church,* NCLS Research, Strathfield, 2009 (accessed 28 November 2012): ncls.org.au/default.aspx?sitemapid=23

17   D Marr, quoted in *Religious Belief in Australia,* podcast, Centre for Public Christianity, Sydney, 27 January 2010 (accessed 28 November 2010): cpx.podbean.com/2010/01/27/david-marr-religious-belief-in-australia

Christians but didn't go to church, would that matter? Would they miss anything? After all, they have access to a Bible, so they don't need church for that. And thanks to the internet, they can podcast the finest preachers in the world, they can YouTube the best praise music in the world, and they can download the best liturgy in the world. In the 21st century, with a reasonable internet connection, you can have music by Hillsong, sermons by Tim Keller and liturgy from *The Book of Common Prayer* —all without leaving your bed. Why, in this golden age, would you bother with church?

Fifty years ago, there were more people who went to church than believed in Jesus. Now it seems there are more people who believe in Jesus than go to church. Does that matter?

The New Testament's answer is an emphatic "Yes". And our union with Christ is a huge part of the reason. In fact, it's no exaggeration to say that we go to church because we are united to Christ.

The New Testament sees the church as one of the greatest expressions, and certainly the most tangible expression, of our union with Christ. Indeed, the case could be made that union with Christ is fundamentally (rather than derivatively) a corporate idea.

When the New Testament talks about our corporate union with Christ, it uses images like the vine and the branches, a temple or a building, a husband and his bride, and so on. But probably the most central picture is the church as the body of Christ.

The body of Christ in the New Testament

In the book of Acts, do you remember what the risen Jesus said to Paul (then Saul) on the road to Damascus? "Saul, Saul," says Jesus, "why are you persecuting me?" (Acts 9:4). Of course, Paul never persecuted Jesus—never even met him. But in that phrase, you see that Jesus' union with his church is so close that to persecute his church—which is what Paul was doing—*is* to persecute Jesus.

The experience must have stuck with Paul, because the idea that Christ is indivisibly united to his church appears everywhere in his letters. Romans 12:5 says, "we, though many, are one body in Christ". In 1 Corinthians 10:17, speaking about the Lord's Supper Paul says, "we who are many are one body, for we all partake of the one bread".

In Ephesians, the image is everywhere. Paul says that God has appointed Christ as head over everything for the church, which is his body (1:22-23). Jew and Gentile come together in the church to form one body (2:14). Christ gives gifts to the church "for building up the body of Christ" (4:12). Later in the same chapter, Christ is the head of the church, and his people are the body, "joined and held together by every joint with which it is equipped" (4:15-16). Then in chapter 5, Christ is the Saviour of the church, his body (5:23).

Galatians 3:28 likewise affirms the same reality. In Christ, "there is neither Jew nor Greek, there is neither slave nor free, there is no male and female, for you are all one [literally, *one man*] in Christ Jesus".

The Trinity and gifts

One of the fullest treatments of this subject is found in 1 Corinthians 12. The context is a church divided over gifts and spiritual manifestations. And into that context, Paul says this:

> Now there are varieties of gifts, but the same Spirit;
> and there are varieties of service, but the same Lord;
> and there are varieties of activities, but it is the same
> God who empowers them all in everyone. (1 Cor 12:4-6)

Did you notice the pattern? As we saw in chapter 1, God delights in this pattern of unity and diversity, sameness and difference, because it reflects his own trinitarian character.

What is different? The gifts. What is the same? The Lord.

God does not have a one-size-fits-all policy when it comes to the body of Christ and its members. There are different gifts, different services, and different workings. To a congregation in danger of being colonized by one gift (speaking in tongues), Paul's emphasis is on the rich variety of gifts given by the one God.

In the body of Christ, at least four things are clear:

- Firstly, that every Christian is given a manifestation of the Spirit (v. 7).
- Secondly, they are not all the same manifestations. If you ask the question: "What does this manifestation, this showing of the Spirit look like?" Paul replies, "It looks different in every case". The emphasis is on the diversity.

- Thirdly, although the manifestations of the Spirit are diverse, they have one purpose: "To each one is given the manifestation of the Spirit *for the common good*" (v. 7). The gifts distributed by the Holy Spirit are given (to import some language from Ephesians 4 for a moment) *so that* the body of Christ can be built up.
- Fourthly, in verse 11, the Spirit has distributed gifts to each believer just as he determined. He has designed our churches not haphazardly, but intentionally. Our job is not to beat up on ourselves for what we cannot do, nor to admire and exalt ourselves for what we can do—but to work out how the particular manifestation of the Spirit in our lives is for the common good of the church.

The body of Christ

Having unpacked how and why the Spirit gives gifts to every believer, Paul now turns his attention back to our collective union with Christ: "For just as the body is one and has many members, and all the members of the body, though many, are one body, so it is with Christ" (v. 12).

At this point, you might have expected Paul's sentence to read, "just as a body is one, so it is with *church*". But for Paul, so close is the connection with Christ and the church that he can use the word 'Christ' where the referent is obviously the church. That's no problem for Paul— the church *is Christ's body*.

As Christ's body, we are a unity, baptized by the

one Spirit into the one body (v. 13). But we are also a diversity, made up of many parts (v. 14).

This is a comfort to the victims of the conflict in the Corinthian church, those without the favoured gifts: "If the foot should say, 'Because I am not a hand, I do not belong to the body,' that would not make it any less a part of the body" (v. 15). And Paul goes on in verse 17 to point out how absurd it would be for the church to have only one gift: "If the whole body were an eye, where would be the sense of hearing? If the whole body were an ear, where would be the sense of smell?" If the group without the favoured gift gave in and conformed, it would damage the whole body, because, as verse 18 says, "God arranged the members in the body, each one of them, as he chose".

But the comfort to the victims is also a challenge to the perpetrators of the division: "The eye cannot say to the hand, 'I have no need of you,' nor again the head to the feet, 'I have no need of you'" (v. 21).

Then in verses 22-24, Paul makes a daring (and slightly awkward) move:

> The parts of the body that seem to be weaker are indispensible, and on those parts of the body that we think less honourable we bestow the greater honour, and our unpresentable parts are treated with greater modesty, which our more presentable parts do not require.

Paul says, "Think of a human body". There are parts, like our faces and our hands, that we are happy for other people to see. And there are other parts of our bodies that get, shall we say, special treatment. And Paul says that this special treatment is in fact a kind of special honour to the less presentable members.

In our churches there are people who, through genetics and background and education and so on, just don't demand that much. They contribute a lot to the body, and they demand very little from the body. And then there are others who have deep and difficult needs. The worldly way to think is that they are a hassle, and that things would be smoother without them. But in God's economy, he is showing those people special honour.

One possible inference is that in the case of the weakest and most broken members of our churches, their very brokenness *is* their gift to the church—because it is as they gift the church with their brokenness, and as we are drawn out of ourselves to learn to serve them, that we learn how to be the body of Christ.

The church (if by that we mean the frail, institutional, prone-to-sin-and-failure sum total of Christians throughout history) is certainly a mixed bag, to say the least. Things have been said and done by the church that no Christian ought to defend or condone. But the idea of loving Christ and hating the church is a perilous and ultimately impossible situation. The church, primarily that actual local gathering of brothers and sisters in the name of Christ, is his body, united to him. As Paul learned on the road to Damascus, you can't hate *that*—you can't hate *them*—and think it's something Jesus will accept.

Despite sometimes being an impediment to the glory of Christ in the world, the church is destined for ultimate glory. God has purposed that there will be glory for himself in the church and in Christ Jesus (Eph 3:21), that heaven and earth will be united for the church (Eph 1:22), and that the church will one day be a spotless bride prepared for Christ and made beautiful by him (Eph 5:27).

And the truth is that, in reality, most people come to know Christ through the word of truth that they hear *in the context of church*. The unbeliever comes into the church in Corinth and says, "God is really among you" (1 Cor 14:25). 1 Peter 2:9-10 says that we are a holy nation that declares the praises of God. And that is actually most often how it happens. It is possible (though rare) for someone to become a Christian by hearing the word of Christ independently of a Christian community. But mostly, it is the dynamite combination of hearing the word of Christ and seeing the body of Christ in action that creates the conditions for faith.

So why go to church? Answer: Because church is who you are. Church is the most concrete expression of your union with Christ. Church is not about you. Sure, the church service you could pull together with a fast internet connection and a warm cup of milk at home would be pretty sweet, but it wouldn't fit the Bible's picture of church because it wouldn't involve *you* blessing the body of Christ with the particular gift(s) he has given you. And it is as we fulfil that role of blessing the body that we learn most deeply what it is to be connected to Christ—to be his.

Woody Allen once said that 80% of life is just showing up. So, here's a practical suggestion for growing in union with Christ: show up to church. I mean *really* show up. Go expecting to be a gift to the body, to bless the body, to love the body and so to love Christ.

I was following the Twitter feed of a Christian conference recently, and according to the feed, a full one-quarter of delegates left after the sermon and before communion to get back to their cars and beat the rush. Irony much? To leave church before partaking of the one loaf that declares our unity as one body! It is almost a textbook definition of what Paul means in 1 Corinthians 11 when he talks about failing to discern the body of Christ—in this case, judging that a quick trip home trumps sharing communion together.

I don't want to be legalistic. Showing up in a grim spirit of ticking off the box that says 'Attended' is not the idea. And of course, there may be very good reasons to have to leave church early—maybe your wife has just gone into labour. Or maybe Richard Dawkins has just asked to pray with you and his plane leaves in 20 minutes. There may be one or two other good reasons. But on the whole, it is hard to imagine that any of the things we rush to are more important than what we are rushing from—fellowship with Christ's body. The distinction we make between how we treat Christ and how we treat his gathered people is not a distinction that Jesus makes.

According to the New Testament, church takes union with Christ from an invisible truth known by faith to a concrete and this-worldly experience. What sort of union is union with Christ? It is the sort of union that has you eyeballing your fellow brothers and sisters in Christ as, together with one voice, you glorify God (Rom 15:6). Understood this way, church is not something we *have* to do, but something we *get* to do.

Chapter 7

UNION WITH CHRIST, RESURRECTION AND THE END OF THE WORLD

Through neglecting the doctrine of union with Christ, many Christians have a bizarre habit of disconnecting what happened to Jesus with what will happen to us. We believe Jesus was raised bodily from the dead, but somehow when it comes to us we are a little more circumspect. We're not sure what to say. Our souls will float up to heaven? We'll be with God? We will... well, who knows? Paul says that this disconnection makes *no sense* if we are united to Christ, for "if we have been united with him in a death like his, we shall certainly be united with him in a resurrection like his" (Rom 6:5). Our resurrection, through union with his, will be like his.

As a rule, we're much sharper on what being united to Christ in his death means than we are on what being united to him in his resurrection means. After all, the Scripture gives us such vivid explanations of the cross: it's like a sacrifice in the temple, a price paid to release a slave, a ransom paid, or an exchange in a market place. My mind can grab onto those pictures and understand them.

But we need not despair, because in 1 Corinthians 15 Paul gives us a picture of union with Christ's resurrection that is every bit as concrete and graspable.

The orchard

"But in fact Christ has been raised from the dead,
the firstfruits of those who have fallen asleep."
(1 Cor 15:20)

Imagine a farmer looking out over his orchard. The resurrection of Jesus is like the firstfruits of the season. If we dwell on that image for a moment, we can see it means *at least* that Jesus is the best and the first. Rather than scrounging up the final miserable remains of a crop for sacrifice, a Jewish farmer would give his firstfruits to God because they were considered the best. In the same way, Jesus' resurrection is the best. He is the last Adam, the new man, the best of the crop to come. He is

God's new humanity *par excellence*, humanity faithfully bearing God's image. He is humanity with all the sin and death and brokenness taken out of the system.

He is the best, and he is also the beginning. He is the firstfruits *of the harvest to come*. That is, what God has done in raising Jesus, he will also do for us. Look at Jesus and you see our future. The absurdity of the Corinthians' position is that they look at the orchard, they see the peach, and they say, "A peach. Great! I wonder what the rest of the fruit on that tree will be." Paul responds with, "You idiots, they'll be peaches! It's a peach tree!" When we see the resurrection of Jesus and say, "A resurrection. Great! I wonder what God will do with us", Paul says, "You idiots, he's going to do with you the same thing he did with Jesus!" We are united with Jesus in a resurrection like his (Rom 6:5).

The resurrected body

When Paul says the resurrection of Christ means there is a general resurrection on the way, there may be some who find the idea wholly unfamiliar. Others may find it a thrilling relief. But for many, when faced with this doctrine, there is only one possible response: *unbelievable.*

Hearing that the Christian hope is for the resurrection of the dead, one may wonder how any rational person could possibly believe it. Are we saying God is going to drag bodies out of graves? What about bodies in various states of decomposition, or bodies that have been cremated? What about the fact that our bodies are the confluence of atoms and cells that have been members of other bodies? That doesn't sound like a new creation; it sounds like a Zombie hope with all the trappings of a bad horror film.

Luckily enough, this is exactly the issue that Paul addresses in his letter to the Corinthians: "But someone will ask, 'How are the dead raised? With what kind of body do they come?'" (v. 35). There are really two questions here. There is a *how* question: How will this resurrection happen? By what power? By what agency? And there is a *what* question: What sorts of bodies will these bodies be, exactly? As he has done before, Paul gives us a picture to help us get our heads around the idea.

The seed

"You foolish person! What you sow does not come to life unless it dies. And what you sow is not the body that is to be, but a bare kernel, perhaps of wheat or of some other grain" (vv. 36-37). Paul wants to help us think about the relationship between our current body and the resurrection body. To what extent are they the same thing? How are they different? And Paul's answer is that the relationship between this body and that body will be like the relationship between a seed and a plant.

If you knew nothing about seed and plants, you could be forgiven for thinking they had no relationship to each other at all. They initially seem so dissimilar. And Paul here is emphasizing the difference: "You foolish person!" he says. "As if the resurrection of the dead will be God pulling our bodies out of their graves in various states of decomposition. No-one is expecting you to believe that!" God is not in the business of dusting us off and resuming play as normal. As one of the commentators has said, "A seed does not come to life by being dug up, brushed down and restored to its pristine seediness".[18]

So the seed and the plant are unlike each other, but we also know that the seed and the plant are closely connected. Everything that the plant becomes was already in the seed. When a seed becomes a plant, it becomes its 'telos'—its end, its goal. The plant is not the rejection of the seed. When a seed becomes a plant, it is the fulfilment of everything the seed was always meant to be. So it is with the resurrection of our bodies. In verses 38-41, Paul is riffing on the first chapter of Genesis. He thinks about the creation in terms of its 'bodies': "But God gives it a body as he has chosen, and to each kind of seed he gives its own body" (v. 38).

Paul then takes the reader on a trip through the creation: human beings have one kind of body, one kind of flesh; birds have another; fish have another. There are bodies in the heavens—that is, the sky; and there are bodies on the earth. Stars have one kind of splendour, the moon another. And all of these things glorify God by being most properly the thing that they are.

---

18 NT Wright, *The Resurrection of the Son of God,* SPCK, London, 2004, p. 342.

And Paul says, "So it will be with the resurrection of the dead". God is making a new world, a new context for a new humanity. At present, our bodies are made for this world, not that world. Our bodies are perishable, dishonoured, weak and natural—but they will be raised imperishable, glorious, powerful and spiritual (vv. 42-44). Then in verses 45-49, Paul makes this great comparison between the two great bodies of humanity: the body of Adam, and the raised body of Jesus. The first—Adam, the first man—was natural; the second—Jesus, the last man—was spiritual.

And we who bear the image of the earthly man will, at the resurrection, bear the image of the heavenly man. We who were once like Adam will then be like the risen Jesus.

Death and all his friends

"Vanity of vanities, says the Preacher, vanity of vanities! All is vanity" (Eccl 1:2). This message is repeated time and time again in the book of Ecclesiastes. 'Vanity' translates as 'mist' or 'vapour', and the main observation of Ecclesiastes is that life is just like that. Life is misty, vaporous, and it goes quickly. It is hard to hold on to and impossible to build on. While dignity can be found in a life that accepts grace and receives rather than grasps, in the end death swallows up everything.

Back in 1 Corinthians 15, Paul repeats what most people say in the face of life's vaporous nature: "Let us eat and drink, for tomorrow we die" (v. 32). The pattern is simple: life-then-death. It is the only lifestyle of a world without hope. And it often looks like a whole lot of fun—whether it's the more audacious expression in eating, drinking, dancing and partying with chemically-enhanced moods and the pure pursuit of pleasure; or the more respectable life of accumulation, of diligently building a life of comfort, security, possessions, family and a killer superannuation. Whichever it is, those life-styles look like fun, but inside each hides a dark and dirty secret: "Let us eat and drink, *for tomorrow we die*".

Death is like a cruel mafia boss, always there getting a slice of the action. As the experiences roll on and the accumulation grows, death is right there reminding us who is really in charge. Why do you have to party hard *now*? Why do you have to grab that sex, that promotion, that money, that opportunity *now*? Why are people in your workplace so willing to sacrifice other people for the sake of their careers? Because death is in charge, always reminding us: "If you don't grab it now, you never will".

That is the pattern of a world without hope. It is joyful on the outside, but despairing at its core.

Death then life

But in 1 Corinthians 15 Paul proclaims, "Death is swallowed up in victory. O death, where is your victory? O death, where is your sting?" (vv. 54-55).

Death tried to swallow Jesus, and it got swallowed in

the process. The sting of death is that we die as sinners and go to meet the one who cannot tolerate sin. But now the death of Jesus has taken away our sin. And so we will feel death, but like the bite of a scorpion without venom, there is no sting. All that is left is the victory of Jesus. His resurrection, and the resurrection of the dead, brings online a new lifestyle with a new pattern. Life-then-death is replaced with death-then-life.

Look how Paul describes his own life: he is in danger; he dies every day; he fought wild beasts in Ephesus (vv. 30-32). Compared to the pagan world, Paul's life looks like death. It looks like denial and sacrifice, like risk and hardship, like labour and toil and frustration. Not stepping on people, but being stepped on. It's a lifestyle of giving, and not grabbing. Paul lives this way because he knows that he is united to Christ, and as such he expects his life to follow the V-shaped life of Jesus, who, though being in very nature God, made himself nothing, trusting that God would raise him up (cf. Phil 2:5-11). The firstfruits have appeared, and a world that looks like it's dying is about to spring into radical new life. Christianity can look prickly on the outside, while paganism looks so happy. But on the inside of paganism is an unremitting despair, and at the heart of the Christian faith is an unbelievable and unstoppable joy, because Christ is risen—and we are united to him.

Therefore be steadfast...

"Therefore, my beloved brothers, be steadfast, immovable, always abounding in the work of the Lord, knowing that in the Lord your labour is not in vain" (1 Cor 15:58). Paul sees that what flows from the gospel's teaching of the resurrection of the dead, and from our union with the risen Lord, is a steadfast immovability. He means both steadfastness in hope and steadfastness in practice. In hope, Paul wants to bridge this great disconnect in the Corinthians' minds between Jesus' resurrection and theirs. We already know (from verses 1-11) that they are steadfast in their belief in the resurrection of Jesus, but he wants to increase the territory captured in that thought.

As the whole world submits to the terms and conditions set by life-then-death, for Paul, steadfastness in practice means letting nothing move you from that great resurrection lifestyle of death-then-life.

So where do you conform to that old pattern of life-then-death? Perhaps in your working life—are you aware of situations where you are grabbing and grasping? Where you are stepping over people to get what you want? And, honestly, on reflection, where have you fallen into thinking that if it's not yours now, it will never be?

Maybe in your personal life there are points where you are tempted to grab (or are actually grabbing) the sex that you can have now, rather than waiting in faithfulness.

Maybe you can see it in your everyday life: in your approach to food; in the way you binge on TV shows;

in the way you do the dishes—aggressively, resentfully, compulsively. Maybe there are patterns of accumulation and consumption that are clearly being played out on a life-then-death template.

The gospel says more than just, "Don't do that". It actually liberates you to live differently. You get to break that pattern, because in Christ you have been included in that great rebellion against death. Now you can say to Death and the lifestyle it dictates: "I don't buy it. I'm dancing to a different tune."

...always abounding in the work of the Lord

Paul says the Corinthians are to remain steadfast. But secondly, they should be *always abounding in the work of the Lord.*

"The work of the Lord" is, in Paul, a phrase that refers specifically to the sort of work that contributes directly to the kingdom of God. Without overplaying or underplaying what verse 58 actually refers to (paid Christian ministry on the one hand, or any kind of labour at all on the other), it seems to me that Paul is talking about the work we do that is specifically, in the sense of the gospel, for the Lord.

If you are a Christian, you can point to that type of work in your life. It is the work of faithfully sharing the news of Jesus with work friends. It is the work of singing and teaching and encouraging in the body of Christ; the work of service in Sunday school or a Bible study. Paul is saying, "Take that and, in the light of the resurrection of

Jesus and our future hope, give yourself fully to it". That is, passionately, with your whole heart. With single-minded devotion. With everything you've got.

And why give yourself over so fully to the work of the Lord? It is because "in the Lord your labour is not in vain" (v. 58).

Paul identifies something that bucks the trend. He names something in this creation, something in our experience, that cannot be described as vain, meaningless or intangible: our labour in the Lord. I think this is because our labour in the Lord is an investment in the new creation. It's the work that we do to see others won to Christ and established in Christ. It is a work sowing seeds to be harvested in the new creation.

Back in verse 36, Paul says, "What you sow does not come to life unless it dies". Jesus' path to life was through death; our path to new life will also be through the door of death. And that is not only the macro story of our lives; it is also the micro story of Christian service. A man gives up a Friday night of relaxation to lead a group of young people by teaching the gospel. A woman goes to serve God in Jordan, and in doing so dies to all the things she might reasonably expect in Australia: security, a husband, a career path. In all these things, the Christ-pattern is there: death-then-life. In all these things, we are burying worldly ambitions in order to see life in others—because, as the parable tells us, we have found a treasure of great price (Matt 13:45-46).

Christ is risen; the orchard that looks dead in the cold of winter is about to spring to life. The great resurrection hope means everything works in reverse. We endure death, throwing ourselves fully into the work of the Lord, with the promise of life in the new creation. And the work is hard—but it has the inestimable advantage of being eternal. The work is sown in frustration, but will one day be raised in glory. Our union with Christ will see us through, safe and glorified into the new creation.

Appendix

DISCUSSION GUIDE

The questions that follow are designed to help you discuss the content of *One Forever* with others—your spouse, your friends or the small group you meet with at church. Use these questions as a way of talking back over the content of each chapter and encouraging one another to put God's word into practice. Feel free to pick and choose your way through the questions, depending on how much time you have available.

Chapter 1: Glory be to God for dappled things—creation

1. How does Genesis 1 capture the unity and diversity of creation? In what ways do the various aspects of creation belong to each other?

2. In Genesis 2, how does God respond to the aloneness of the man? What does the writer of Genesis draw from this encounter (v. 24)?
3. According to Paul in Ephesians 5, the union of Adam and Eve points to a greater union. To which union does it point? How does the nature of Adam and Eve's union help us to understand the union of Ephesians 5?

A prayer

God our Father, you are the source of the union of all created things, and you purposed the union of the man and the woman in the garden. Delight us, Lord, in that more perfect union for which we are all made—the union of Christ and his church. We ask this in the name of your Son our Lord and our bridegroom, Jesus Christ. Amen.

Chapter 2: Into the far country—incarnation

1. According to the words of the Nicene Creed, why did God become a man?
2. How does the incarnation honour our humanity? How does it challenge our fallen humanity?
3. What does the incarnation of the Son of God say about God's purpose for our future?

A prayer

Almighty God, you have given us your only Son to take our nature upon himself, conceived by the Holy Spirit, born of Mary. Grant to us that we might be daily renewed by your Holy Spirit through the Lord Jesus Christ, who now lives and reigns with you, the one mediator between God and man. Amen.

Chapter 3: In Christ you are a new creation—salvation

1. List some of the images the New Testament uses to capture our union with Christ. What are they trying to capture?
2. How would you describe the idea of being 'in Christ' to someone new to the concept?
3. What does it mean for us to be 'in Adam'? What is made possible for us now that we are 'in Christ'?

A prayer

God our Father, you have rescued us from judgement in the First Adam by including us by faith in the Last Adam, Jesus Christ. Grant us, Lord, the assurance of faith and knowledge of our sure salvation in him. We ask through Jesus Christ our Lord, amen.

Chapter 4: Before the throne of God above—justification

1. What does it mean to be justified before God?
2. How does being in Christ establish our justification?
3. According to Romans 8, what could undo our status before God? Why?

A prayer

Almighty God, through the death and resurrection of your Son you have made it possible for us to be justified before you. Grant to us that we would live joyfully and obediently in the knowledge that there is therefore now no condemnation for those who are in Christ Jesus. We ask in his name, amen.

Chapter 5: In which we face some playground bullies—sin and union

1. How does our union with Christ shape our relationship with sin? (See Romans 6:1-10.)
2. What do we need to do in the light of what has been done for us? (See Romans 6:11-14.)
3. How, in your own words, does the fact of union with Christ make a difference in the actual encounter with temptation?

A prayer

God our Father, you have included us in the death and resurrection of Jesus so that what is true of him is now true of us. Grant us therefore, gracious Lord, the courage and strength to not let sin reign in our bodies, knowing that we stand in your grace. We ask through Jesus Christ our Lord, amen.

Chapter 6: United to the body of Christ—church

1. According to 1 Corinthians 12:4-6, what do we as Christians share in common? What makes us diverse?
2. What is God's purpose for our diversity? (See 1 Corinthians 12:7-11.)
3. How might an understanding of your local church as the body of Christ change your attitude toward it and ministry within it?

A prayer

Almighty God, in uniting us to Christ you have also united to us his body, the church. Help us, Lord, to be faithful servants of your church, allowing the gifts you have given us to be used for the building up of Christ's body. This we ask in the name of Jesus, to whom be glory forever. Amen.

Chapter 7: Union with Christ, resurrection and the end of the world

1. What does it mean for Christ in his resurrection to be "the firstfruits of those who have fallen asleep" (1 Cor 15:20)? What will happen to our bodies on the last day?

2. How does a life shaped by future resurrection differ from a life in which death is the end?

3. Paul calls for us to be "abounding in the work of the Lord" (1 Cor 15:58). What is the "work of the Lord"? What would it look like to abound in it? Why is the work of the Lord "not in vain"?

A prayer

God our Father, through the resurrection of Jesus you have released us from a life of slavery to death. Help us, Lord, to abound in your work, knowing that the work of the Lord is not in vain. This we ask in the name of Jesus Christ, who has conquered death and who lives and reigns with you and the Holy Spirit, one God forever and ever. Amen.

Feedback on this resource

We really appreciate getting feedback about our resources—not just suggestions for how to improve them, but also positive feedback and ways they can be used. We especially love to hear that the resources may have helped someone in their Christian growth.

You can send feedback to us via the 'Feedback' menu in our online store, or write to us at info@matthiasmedia.com.au.

❀matthiasmedia

Matthias Media is an evangelical publishing ministry that seeks to persuade all Christians of the truth of God's purposes in Jesus Christ as revealed in the Bible, and equip them with high-quality resources, so that by the work of the Holy Spirit they will:

- abandon their lives to the honour and service of Christ in daily holiness and decision-making
- pray constantly in Christ's name for the fruitfulness and growth of his gospel
- speak the Bible's life-changing word whenever and however they can—in the home, in the world and in the fellowship of his people.

Our wide range of resources includes Bible studies, books, training courses, tracts and children's material. To find out more, and to access samples and free downloads, visit our website:

www.matthiasmedia.com

How to buy our resources

1. Direct from us over the internet:
   – in the US: www.matthiasmedia.com
   – in Australia: www.matthiasmedia.com.au

2. Direct from us by phone: please visit our website for current phone contact information.

3. Through a range of outlets in various parts of the world. Visit **www.matthiasmedia.com/contact** for details about recommended retailers in your part of the world.

4. Trade enquiries can be addressed to:
   – in the US and Canada: sales@matthiasmedia.com
   – in Australia and the rest of the world: sales@matthiasmedia.com.au

Register at our website for our **free** regular email update to receive information about the latest new resources, **exclusive special offers**, and free articles to help you grow in your Christian life and ministry.

Also by Rory Shiner

so by Rory Shiner and Peter Orr

The World Next Door
A short guide to the Christian faith

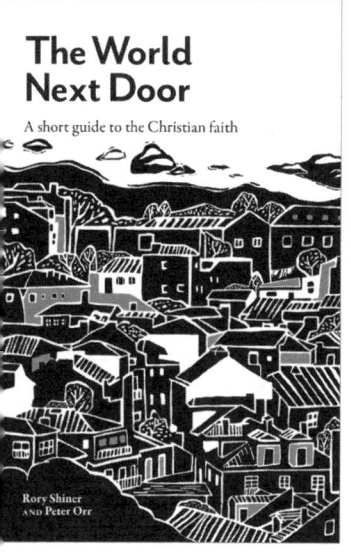

"This book is our best shot at commending the Christian message to our friends and neighbours. It's driven by the universal human instinct to increase the joy of finding a good thing by sharing it with others. We both think we've found a good thing—the best thing—in finding God through Jesus. We want to share it."

Taking the ancient but timeless Apostles' Creed as their starting point, pastor Rory Shiner and atheist-turned-theologian Peter Orr introduce you to the fundamentals of the Christian faith. Fast-paced, entertaining, personal, and compelling, *The World Next Door* invites you into a world where Jesus Christ reigns supreme and where lives are changed forever.